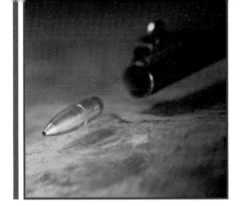

School Shootings and School Violence

A Hot Issue

Bárbara C. Cruz

HOT ISSUES

Enslow Publishers, Inc.

40 Industrial Road	PO Box 38
Box 398	Aldershot
Berkeley Heights, NJ 07922	Hants GU12 6BP
USA	UK

http://www.enslow.com

*For Ivonne Blank and Judy Hanson, two fine educators
who continue to positively influence children's lives with
their wisdom, patience, and love*

Library of Congress Cataloging-in-Publication Data

Cruz, Bárbara C.
   School shootings and school violence : a hot issue / Bárbara C. Cruz.
      p. cm. — (Hot issues)
   Includes bibliographical references and index.
   Summary: Discusses the problem of violence in schools, citing cases of
   shootings at Columbine High School and others, and suggests possible
   reasons for these incidents as well as some of the ways schools have
   reacted to them.
   ISBN 0-7660-1813-X (hardcover)
   1. School shootings—Juvenile literature. 2. School
   violence—Juvenile literature. [1. School shootings. 2. School violence.
   3. Violence.] I. Title. II. Series.
   LB3013.3 .C78 2002
   373.17'82—dc21
                              2001008103

Printed in the United States of America

10 9 8 7 6 5 4 3 2 1

To Our Readers: We have done our best to make sure all Internet Addresses in
this book were active and appropriate when we went to press. However, the
author and the publisher have no control over and assume no liability for the
material available on those Internet sites or on other Web sites they may link to.
Any comments or suggestions can be sent by e-mail to comments@enslow.com
or to the address on the back cover.

Illustration Credits: AP/Wide World Photos: pp. 6, 8, 13, 34, 41, 51;
Corbis Images Royalty-Free, p. 1; Mary O'Connor, p. 22; Skjold
Photographs, pp. 14, 30.

Cover Illustrations: EyeWire Images (background); Hemera
Technologies, Inc. (inset).

Contents

Author's Note

In *School Shootings and School Violence*, the author has opted to leave out specific names of the perpetrators of school violence. The reason behind this choice lies in the issue of copycat crimes. The latest Secret Service report indicates that many school shooters have claimed "becoming famous" as one of their prime motives. One suggestion that has been made to the media has been to minimize glorification of such individuals by omitting their names in vehicles such as newspaper articles and broadcast news pieces.

The author would like to recognize the following individuals for their support and encouragement: Aimee Fogelman, for her thorough research skills; Christiana Schumann, for sharing resources and insights; Lisa Keigher, whose informal discussions led to a deeper understanding of the issues; and manuscript reviewers, for their thoughtful and helpful comments.

Chapter 1

A Growing Concern

The morning of April 20, 1999, began typically enough at Columbine High School in Littleton, Colorado. But at around 11:30 A.M., two male students dressed in military fatigues and ankle-length black trench coats walked onto the school parking lot. Underneath their coats they carried a deadly arsenal: a pistol, a rifle, and two sawed-off shotguns. Police later found more than thirty pipe bombs as well.

The two students—one seventeen years old, one eighteen years old—were part of a group of students called the "Trench Coat Mafia." That morning they fired as they entered the school and walked toward the cafeteria. Students ran toward exits or hid. The killers continued shooting as they went to the second-floor library.

After a tense four hours, the killers were found in the school's library, dead from gunshot wounds to the head. The rampage left fourteen students and one teacher dead and another twenty-two wounded. It was the deadliest episode of school violence on record.

The grisly tragedy was to be repeated exactly one month later at Heritage High School in Conyers, Georgia.

On May 20, 1999, a fifteen-year-old boy opened fire in his school, shooting six of his classmates. He had bragged to a friend that he could do better than the Columbine gunmen. The shooter's friend, a Heritage High freshman, remembered, "He said it should have happened to our school a long time ago."[1]

Across the nation, bewildered Americans discussed and debated what could be done to curb school violence. As a result of Columbine and other school shootings, educators expanded their definition of school violence. The term now includes both criminal acts and aggressive behavior that prevents learning and harms the school climate.

Experts are not sure how a tragedy such as the one that happened in Littleton can be prevented. A risk manager with the public schools in Denver, Colorado,

*S*tudents sing hymns during a candlelight service for the victims of the shooting at Santana High School that left two dead and thirteen wounded.

says, "Short of making our schools fortresses with moats and drawbridges, I just don't know what to do. I'm at a loss."[2]

The public has grown frightened and weary. Towns such as West Paducah, Kentucky; Jonesboro, Arkansas; Pearl, Mississippi; and Springfield, Oregon, are now associated with school tragedies. Long identified with inner cities, people now realize that violence and school shootings are just as likely to happen in small towns and in suburban settings. President Clinton remarked, "Perhaps now America will wake up to the dimensions of this challenge, if it could happen in a place like Littleton."[3]

Far from being an inner-city problem, school violence can and does happen everywhere. Violence has even been declared a "public health emergency."[4] According to Youth Crime Watch, 3 million crimes are committed on school grounds every year. And in the United States, teens are the victims of more crimes than any other age group.[5] The crisis has led to a new job: school risk managers, experts who predict and try to prevent violence and crises in schools.

While they are still rare, the number of multiple-victim homicides in schools has increased over the years.[6] Multiple-victim homicides refer to events where the offender killed more than one person. Since 1978 there have been at least two dozen school shootings resulting in deaths.

Following the Littleton tragedy, there were even reports of an increase in home schooling. The Colorado Department of Education's home-schooling department, for example, reported a 60 percent increase in the number of calls.[7] Brian Rohrbough, whose fifteen-year-old son, Daniel, was among those murdered at Columbine, remembers people saying, "If my child is O.K., he or she will never set foot in that school again."[8]

The Columbine shootings had an impact not just in Colorado, however. The effects were immediately felt around the nation. Violence intervention programs were started. Anonymous hot lines for reporting possible violence were created. "Zero tolerance" policies—strict rules and punishments—were implemented. And across the nation, schools scrambled to strengthen security. According to one study, public schools are now spending about $795 million on security each year.[9]

Students across the nation think about such a tragedy happening in their school. Middle school student Jess Kramer said, "At lunch we would talk about what we would do if it happened to us—would we go out this door and stuff like that. The idea of someone coming in with a bomb made us really, really scared."[10]

Parents, educators, students and communities search actively for solutions for the growing and troubling problem of school violence. But many believe that before we find solutions we must figure out what causes the problem. What causes this small minority of teens to lash out against their peers and against society?

*I*n Springfield, Oregon, students embrace in a group hug before entering school for the first time after a shooting spree in which two students were killed.

Chapter 2

The Nagging Question: Why?

Whenever there is news that a school shooting has occurred, the first question asked is "Why?" People, dazed by the shock of the event, struggle to find answers. Experts try to address the prevention of such violence and also figure out what caused it to begin with. A number of reasons have been offered: the decline of the family unit, parenting that is too permissive, the growth of gangs, access to alcohol, drugs, and guns, and violent images and messages in the media and popular culture.

Most experts warn against pointing fingers at any one cause. Rather, the *combination* of factors and risks is likely the culprit. Child psychologist James Garbarino is a Cornell University professor and author of *Lost Boys: Why Our Sons Turn Violent and How We Can Save Them*. He says: "Television, video games, movies, guns, child maltreatment, unresponsive schools, inadequate mental services, spiritual emptiness, psychoactive substances, economic inequality; is there anyone among us without responsibility?"[1]

There does not seem to be a specific pattern associated with school violence and shootings. However, experts usually point to two general factors that seem to provide some clues: conditions that breed or allow violence and individual personalities. Psychologists say that the complex interaction of the two most likely explains—and may even predict—violent behavior.

Home and Family

Many people feel that there has been a breakdown of the family unit in our society. Adult contact with children seems to be decreasing just when it may be most needed. The National School Safety Center (NSSC) reports that youth involved in school-related deaths often had little or no supervision or support from parents or a caring adult. The NSSC also found that many of these violent kids had witnessed or been a victim of abuse or neglect in their homes.[2]

There are some home environments that seem to encourage violence. Studies have found that availability of weapons, problematic parenting, and weak family bonds can all contribute to violence in children.[3] As a result, some violence intervention programs target home life in order to improve student behavior. Tom DeCair, the spokesman for the Josephson Institute of Ethics, points out, "Parents are the first line of defense in building a kid's character."[4] Having positive role models tends to reduce the occurrence of bullying.[5]

Many experts believe that parental actions—or the lack of them—are key to molding a child. L. Alan Sroufe, a researcher at the University of Minnesota, studied 175 people from birth to age twenty-three. He concludes "that nothing is more important for the child's development than the quality of (parental) care received."[6] Another researcher, Kenneth Dodge of Duke University, is following nine hundred youngsters as part of a study on aggression and violence. So far, he has found that changing aggressive parenting behaviors, such as spanking and verbal abuse, can significantly reduce aggressive behavior in kids.[7]

Availability of Guns

Some people feel that part of the school violence problem is the number of guns owned by private citizens. There are an estimated 200 million handguns in the United States, and gun violence costs Americans over $2 billion annually in physical injuries alone.[8] Each year, 35,000 people die from a gunshot.[9]

Teenagers are not immune. A 2001 study found that almost 50 percent of American high school students have easy access to guns. The survey also found that one in five high school boys took a weapon to school the previous year.[10] Although juveniles are not permitted to buy or own guns, it can be very easy for a troubled youth to get one. In most school violence cases, the shooter stole a family gun. According to the Center to Prevent Handgun Violence, there are two guns for every household in the United States. Youngsters can also acquire guns illegally from sellers who probably stole the firearms. In some communities kids can even "rent" a gun for a period of time, paying an hourly or daily fee for its use.

Because of the increase in the number of handguns in society, some of the antiviolence legislation has focused on decreasing the number of weapons as well as making it tougher to buy one.

Poverty and Neglect

When six-year-old Kayla Rolland was shot and killed by a boy in her first grade class, the nation was almost as sad for the six-year-old boy who pulled the trigger as for the victim. Arthur Busch, the county prosecutor in Mount Morris Township, Michigan, said: "That boy is an absolute victim of his environment."[11] The boy was too young to be charged in the tragedy, but his nineteen-year-old uncle, who owned the stolen gun, was charged with manslaughter. The child's mother, a drug addict, was charged with neglect. The boy's father was in jail. The boy and his eight-year-old brother had shared a single sofa as their bed.

Trash was strewn throughout the yard and inside the house, which was used as a meeting point for drug deals. Neighbors said that drugs and guns had been a part of the young killer's everyday life.

Concerned citizens point out the connections between poverty, drugs, and violence. Poverty has been linked with 85 percent of gun deaths among young people.[12] Film director Michael Moore, who made a famous documentary about the decline of the auto industry in Michigan, said: "When you put abject [hopeless] poverty together with easy access to guns, you have a recipe for this kind of violence."[13]

Teasing and Taunting

Adolescence is a difficult time period for most students. It can be especially hard if one is constantly teased or bullied. Bullying refers to students who pick on others or make others do things against their will (for example, give them money or personal property). Bullying goes beyond simple teasing and makes the school climate fearful and intimidating.[14] Approximately 15 percent of students are regularly targeted by bullies or are themselves bullies.[15] A 1999 study by the U.S. Department of Education found that bullying occurs most during the middle school years.[16]

Psychologist Dorothy Espelage has studied bullying, and she has concluded that it can have serious consequences. The teasing and harassing can leave kids feeling depressed, anxious, and apt "to do to someone else what has been done to them."[17] A study by the Secret Service released in 2000 revealed that in two thirds of the school shooting incidents, the shooters felt bullied, threatened, or attacked by other students before the shooting.[18]

Rejection or maltreatment by schoolmates can leave deep wounds. Augustana University professor Larry Brendtro says, "Kids who feel powerless and rejected are capable of doing horrible things."[19] The link between being bullied and hurting others is so strong that the National School Safety Center has it on its checklist of characteristics of kids who have caused school deaths. In most of the recent school shootings, the shooters had been picked on by peers. One study found that by the age of twenty-four, 60 percent of those who had been bullies in school had at least one criminal conviction.[20]

Constant teasing and bullying were part of the explanation given for why a fifteen-year-old boy killed two fellow students and wounded thirteen people at his high school in Santee, California. Classmates told of how the boy was regularly teased for being small for his age. Bullies had stolen his skateboard and his shoes. Bullies had even pressed a still-hot lighter to his neck. Just one week before the shooting, the fifteen-year-old had sent an e-mail message to a friend saying that he was fearful of going to school.[21]

Several states and school districts are devoting funding to solve the problem. Massachusetts has committed a million dollars for antibullying programs. In Colorado, lawmakers passed legislation requiring school districts to have a policy directed at student bullying. Colorado Senate Bill 80 mandates an antibullying program in every school. Other states are looking at similar proposals.

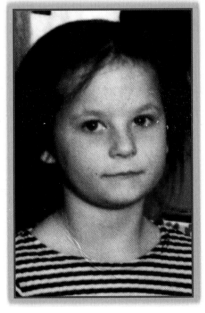

*F*irst-grader Kayla Rolland was killed when another six-year-old brought his uncle's gun to school.

Isolation and Alienation

Often, it is young people who can best help in providing an understanding. They can point out the students who seem disconnected, angry, or withdrawn. Students who are socially alienated are the most likely to be involved in school violence. Some are hostile to peers, openly aggressive, and antisocial. They tend to be rejected by their peers and are uninvolved in school affairs.

These students often store their pain in silence, quietly building up rage. Although some kids might keep their hurt inside, others might turn it outward, leading to violence against others. Seventeen-year-old Columbine student Wes Lammers remembers that he and his peers were aware of "the dark side" of the Trench Coat Mafia. Wes says, "There were a lot of jokes that one day they might snap or something."[22]

*S*tudents who feel alienated and depressed are more likely than others to be involved in school violence.

Many troubled youth also feel alienated from their parents. Most violent teens are disrespectful to authority figures (such as teachers, parents, and police) and are directly defiant of school rules and norms. Often, alienated students get together and form a subculture where they find acceptance from each other. They may then, in turn, reject traditional values and customs and embrace delinquent or illegal ones. They may join a gang or become involved in drugs or alcohol. Fifteen-year-old Jason Sanchez understands how a teenager can "snap." Jason says, "If you go to school, and people make fun of you every day, and you don't have friends, it drives you to insanity."[23]

Just as disturbing are those students who are ignored by their peers. The sixteen-year-old Pearl High School student who opened fire in his Mississippi school, killing two students and wounding seven others, said that he "felt like nobody cared." When interviewed by the Secret Service, he said, "I just didn't have anyone to talk to about all the things I was going through. I kept a lot of hurt inside me."[24] Psychologist Robert Brooks says, "A common thing among the school shooters is a feeling of isolation. The more you're isolated, the more impossible life is."[25]

Gender

Interestingly, almost all the students involved in the high-profile school shootings since 1978 have been male. In fact, males are much more likely than females to be aggressive at school and to be the victim of violence. In a national study of deaths on school campuses, it was found that nine out of the ten deaths involved a male as both the perpetrator and the victim.[26] Boys are also much more likely to bring a gun or other weapon to school.[27]

In seeking to explain why males tend to act more aggressively than females, one theory is that girls and boys are brought up very differently. While girls are encouraged to talk about their feelings, boys are usually taught to act out their emotions. Over time, boys may become unable to express their feelings with words and turn to violence instead.

But attention is now starting to be focused on violent girls as well. More girls are involved in violent crime than they were a decade ago. Since then, for example, the arrest rate for murder among girls has risen 64 percent.[28] When a fourteen-year-old shot a classmate at her school in Williamsport, Pennsylvania, in March 2001, part of the reason it made national headlines was that the shooter was a girl. Violence prevention programs are acknowledging that the problem no longer just affects boys. One expert says, "We're teaching violence in our society and we're making lethal weapons available to young people.... Girls, after all, are people. And many of these responses are human."[29]

The Media

For years educators and psychologists have warned that television violence contributes to aggression in children. Recent studies seem to confirm these fears. By some estimates, the typical American child is exposed to 200,000 acts of television violence by the age of eighteen.[30] Repeated exposure to violence may not just make children and teens more aggressive, it may also numb them to violent acts.

Hollywood has also received a flood of criticism. The biggest box office hits are often violent films with elaborate explosions and other high-tech effects. When it was reported that one of the two Columbine killers had closely watched *Natural Born Killers*, Hollywood was again inundated with accusations.

Just how big an impact do the media have on kids? Do television and video games really have an influence on teens' behavior? And can the media also help in discouraging future tragedies?

Chapter 3

The Media: Friend or Foe?

By the year 2000, Americans had become weary of hearing about yet another school shooting on the evening news. But the one that occurred on February 29 of that year in Mount Morris Township, Michigan, was particularly shocking. Following a playground squabble the day before, a six-year-old boy shot and killed classmate Kayla Rolland in their first-grade classroom. The boy became the youngest school killer in the nation's history.

As people struggled to understand the tragedy, attention turned to the young killer's home life. One of the details picked up by the news services was the boy's television viewing habits. The boy's father, who was serving time in jail, admitted that his son spent much of his time "watching violent movies and TV."[1]

Del Elliott, the director of the Center for the Study and Prevention of Violence at the University of Colorado, believes today's kids "are exposed to [a higher] level of violence than any other generation we know of."[2] Many people believe that part of the reason for that is the number of violent images and messages we are exposed to every day through the media. A 1999 study found that, on average, children spend more than five hours daily watching television, playing video games, and involved in other media.[3] More than 50 percent of kids have television sets in their bedrooms.[4]

Spending a lot of time watching television or playing video games also takes away time from being with friends and family, playing outside, and doing schoolwork. Today's teens spend much of their time away from grown-ups. Hill Walker, codirector of the Institute on Violence and Destructive Behavior in Oregon, says that many teenagers' lives are "almost a virtual reality without adults."[5]

Much of the concern with so much interaction with media is exposure to violence. Professor John Martin Rich believes, "Children can come away from a violent program with the idea that violence is an easy solution for everyday problems or a smart, efficient way to handle difficult people."[6] Among the characteristics the National School Safety Center targets as warning behaviors for school violence is preferring television shows, music, and films that have violent themes and acts. The executive director of the National Institute on Media and the Family says, "There is a great deal of violence in our media. It creates an atmosphere in which violent behavior is more likely to occur."[7] Researchers at Stanford University found that students whose exposure to television and videos has been limited act less aggressively toward their peers and on the school playground.[8]

News Programs

The media have also been blamed for their sensationalistic response to the school shooting tragedies and their exaggeration of youth crime and school violence. People complain that evening news programs are often filled with only pessimistic stories of violence and death. Television news shows have been criticized for emphasizing the shock value of school shootings and perhaps even inciting copycat crimes.

Yet several organizations studying the problem report that the number of violent acts in schools is actually lower than ever. More than 99.99 percent of public schools have never even had a homicide.[9]

Department of Justice statistics show that violent juvenile crime has decreased since the early 1990s.[10] According to the Justice Department, the murder arrest rate for juveniles reached its peak in 1993. Since then, it has steadily declined, plunging 68 percent by 1999.[11] Today, there is less violence committed by juveniles both in and out of school than there was a decade ago.

Despite all the reports of random acts of violence in schools, schools are among the safest places to be in this country. In the federal government's annual report on school safety, it was found that less than one percent of the children who were murdered or committed suicide were at school. Most school crime is theft, the report revealed, not serious violent crime.[12] While school shootings make the evening news, school administrators report being much more concerned about daily problems such as vandalism and fights between students.[13]

In another report, *School House Hype*, the Justice Policy Institute found that 90 percent of juvenile killings actually occur at home. Vincent Schiraldi, director of the institute, blames media coverage for creating the misunderstanding that schools are a dangerous place for children. He says, "If we want to reduce the overall number of childhood gun deaths we should be expanding after-school programs and restricting gun sales."[14]

Movies

The fourteen-year-old boy who killed three classmates and wounded five others at his school in West Paducah, Kentucky, told investigators that he had watched the movie *The Basketball Diaries*. During a dream sequence in the film, teens with guns take over their high school. In

Selected Statistics on School Violence

- In the last half of the 1990s, there was a steady decline from 17% to 12% in the proportion of students in grades nine through twelve who reported carrying a weapon to school on one or more days during the previous month.

- Physical attacks without a weapon, theft, and vandalism are much more common in schools than are more serious incidents.

- There are one hundred times more guns in the hands of children attending American schools than principals have been reporting to Congress.

- 37% of students reported a gang presence at their school.

- 44% of students say they feel "a lot" of responsibility for keeping their schools safe.

- Larger schools are more likely to report a criminal incident to police than small schools.

- Students are twice as likely to be victims of serious violent crime away from school as at school.

- Nearly 5% of students aged 12-18 reported being bullied at school in the last six months.

- About 20% of both middle and high schools report at least one serious violent crime.

Source: Adapted from "Stats 2000: Selected School Violence Research Findings," Fall 2000, *Center for the Prevention of School Violence Page*, <www.ncsu.edu/cpsv/Acrobatfiles/2000%20statistics.PDF> (September 6, 2001).

the movie, actor Leonardo DiCaprio, dressed in a black trench coat, opens fire and kills six students and his teacher. Attorney Tim Kaltenbach said of the fourteen-year-old shooter, "It was a factor in his mind. I believe it's fair to take him at his word."[15]

James Garbarino says he would like to see media violence treated as a public health problem. He likens it to treating an infectious disease like cholera. Just as sewage treatment plants have to be treated at the source to reduce a contagious disease, he says, Hollywood has to be looked at as a source of media violence.[16] Some shooting victims and their families have even started suing moviemakers, alleging that Hollywood movies may have provoked troubled youths to go on shooting sprees.

Video and Computer Games

Video games like Tomb Raider, Mortal Kombat, and Doom have also received their share of blame for teen violence. Shooting victims and their families have also started suing video game manufacturers, saying that they teach and provoke people to kill. Parents of several victims in the West Paducah, Kentucky, school shooting filed a lawsuit against twenty-five media and entertainment companies. And some experts predict that the Littleton families will sue the maker of Doom, a violent video game that the two Columbine killers reportedly played obsessively.[17]

Researchers have found that violent video games may actually be more damaging than television and film violence. Students were first evaluated to determine their existing levels of anger and irritability. Then, half the students played violent video games while the other half played nonviolent ones. Players of the violent games showed an increase in aggressive thoughts and behavior. And those who had originally measured higher in anger and irritability had even higher increases in aggression after playing the violent games.[18]

Experts believe that part of the reason why the games

*M*any experts believe that violent computer games and exposure to inappropriate material on the Internet contribute to violent behavior.

may be more harmful is that they are interactive. By learning to shoot at people in virtual reality, critics argue, children might learn to be violent in real life.[19]

The Internet

Although the Internet has brought wonderful opportunities and exchange of information to millions of people, it can also be a source of misinformation and violent messages. Racist and violent hate groups have Web sites encouraging hurtful thought and behavior. And with an estimated 11 million teenagers now online, there is a good chance that they will be exposed to inappropriate material.

Some people even believe that the hate groups target bright, college-bound teens. Mark Potok of the Southern Poverty Law Center, which monitors hate groups in the

United States, believes, "The Net has proved to be very useful for these groups in reaching what they see as the future leaders of tomorrow. Do they target kids? Yeah, I think so."[20]

Some teens have even been able to download bomb-making plans from the World Wide Web. When police searched the bedroom of the fifteen-year-old boy who shot six of his classmates in Conyers, Georgia, they found three pages of bomb-building instructions printed from the Internet. Although the student never carried out his plan of planting bombs, he was able to bring a rifle and handgun into his school.

There is also the problem of students harassing each other via computer. There is a growing number of reports of taunting and bullying online. On many Web sites, teens can log on in chat rooms using fake names and write almost anything they want. According to the Student Press Law Center, at least half of all American high schools have "underground" Web sites. That means that there are at least ten thousand secret sites in the United States where students post messages, rumors, and images. These Web sites are not officially affiliated with a school and are usually unknown to school administrators or parents. Students can post any message they want. One girl even posted a "hit list" of students at her school who she thought should die.[21]

Popular Music and Song Lyrics

Reportedly, members of the Trench Coat Mafia at Columbine High School were avid fans of shock rockers Marilyn Manson and Nine Inch Nails. Although later reports contradicted initial rumors, Marilyn Manson in particular received his fair share of blame in the tragedy. Manson remembers, "There were a lot of death threats after Columbine. I wasn't sure how safe I was because there were a lot of people who had laid blame on me for something that I wasn't responsible for."[22]

Of course, not everyone believes that music can turn

someone into a killer. Rock musician Alice Cooper says that music is "just the easiest target. It's the music and the video games—that must be it. If that's true, then why didn't every other kid at . . . Columbine High School in Colorado kill everybody? They all played the same games, watched the same movies and listened to the same albums. Why just these two guys?"[23]

Marilyn Manson, who has been interviewed dozens of times since the Columbine shootings, feels it is unfair to blame the group—or rock music in general—for the tragedy. Manson says: "You can't blame people's behavior on books, music, film and video games, which are important outlets for emotions. Growing up, I always escaped to music if things got too hard to deal with. When you take away the things people identify with, you create these little time bombs that eventually explode. People feel smothered when they aren't heard."[24]

Rap music has also been condemned for encouraging violence. Parents, educators, and some students are alarmed by increasingly violent images and messages. Much of the criticism focuses on gangsta rap, a type of rap that describes the dismal daily violence in many U.S. cities. Gangsta rap gained notoriety in 1992 with rapper Ice-T's song "Cop Killer." Since then, rappers such as Snoop Dogg, Dr. Dre, and DMX have also been criticized for inciting violence. Some people argue that the music glorifies violence and may provoke impressionable kids to be violent. In 1991, five Kansas teens pleaded not guilty to murder, claiming a rap record made them insane.[25]

But others defend the musical style, saying that it merely reflects the dire conditions from which the rappers come and that it may provide a much-needed outlet for frustrated youth. And many teens indignantly point out that they know the difference between fantasy and reality.

The Media—A Friend?

Aside from the negative implications, can the media also play a positive role in preventing future tragedies?

One of the most controversial research findings has been the idea that media violence can have a cathartic effect. (Catharsis usually refers to ridding oneself of undesirable emotions.) Could it be that by watching or interacting with violent media, some kids might actually "get it out of their system" and be less aggressive?[26]

The media can also dispense accurate information and dispel fears and rumors. In addition, news writers can use the tragedies to compose pieces that help families communicate about the issues.

The media have also been asked to be discreet when reporting school shooting tragedies. When covering the shooting in Santee, California, on March 5, 2001, several television stations minimized on-air time devoted to the event. News reporters and photographers have also been asked to be sensitive to victims after a tragedy. After the May 21, 1998, school shooting in Springfield, Oregon, the *Chicago Sun-Times* kept the tragic story off the front page. A notice to readers explained that it was to protect children and to avoid giving unstable teens any violent ideas.

The makers of major motion pictures have been challenged to create movies that realistically portray violence and do not glorify it. That way, the theory goes, people will better understand violence's real effects. Film and television writers are also being asked to develop scripts that show how problems can be resolved nonviolently.

Some people worry that the real danger is not in the media paying too much attention to school violence, but giving it too little consideration as it becomes more common. Walter Isaacson, managing editor of *Time* magazine, says, "The more information we have about these cases, and the more we discuss the issues, the better."[27]

Chapter 4

Gangs, Cults, Drugs, and Alcohol

The Trench Coat Mafia was the subject of much discussion following the shooting tragedy at Columbine High School. The group was made up of fifteen to twenty students who were rejected by the popular kids at school. The group members seemed to pride themselves on being different and "being on the fringe." They often sat in the back of the class and sometimes did not answer when spoken to. Other times, they scared classmates when they started voicing their hatred for African Americans, Hispanics, and Jews.[1] Almost immediately, news reports began to connect the group to the shooting.

When the National School Safety Center (NSSC) reviewed school deaths from 1992 to 2000, the organization turned its attention to the youngsters who caused the deaths. After looking at all the tragic incidents, the NSSC compiled a checklist of common characteristics. Several of the warning behaviors had to do with participation in gangs and fringe groups and use of illegal substances. One study investigated alienated high school students who were identified as "troublemakers." The researchers found that the problematic students were often involved in gangs, abused drugs, and used weapons.[2]

Michael Josephson, the president of the Josephson Institute of Ethics, sums it up this way: "Today's teens, especially boys, have a high propensity to use violence when they are angry, they have easy access to guns, drugs and alcohol, and a disturbing number take weapons to school."[3]

Just how influential are gangs, fringe groups, and cults? And is there a connection between school violence and illegal substances?

Cliques and Fringe Groups

Ask parents and educators to name the strongest influence on teens and most will reply "their peers." Some research studies indicate that not only is that the case, but also that parents and schools may be able to have very little impact on young people.[4] Controversial author Judith Harris has a theory that peers, more than parents or schools, have the greatest influence on the personality development of a child. She cites, for example, teen smoking. The best predictor of teen smoking is not whether the teen's parents smoke, but whether the teen's friends smoke.

Cliques refer to people who form groups based on common interests or activities. The cliques evident in American high schools are well-known: athletes, cheerleaders, clean-cut "preppies," and studious "nerds." Sometimes there are also gangbangers, gothics, and white supremacists. In some schools students group themselves according to the music they listen to: rock, rap, country music, and top 40.

For some students, all their socializing is done within the confine of their clique. They rarely associate with others outside their group. As one senior high student explains, "Think of us as living in a lot of different bubbles."[5]

Cliques are powerful because they can give kids a sense of belonging. Such was the case of the lone shooter in the Santana High tragedy. Bullied in school, disconnected from his mother, neglected by his father, the fifteen-year-old found a group that would have him: a band of skateboarders who hung out at a neighborhood park, doing drugs and drinking alcohol.[6] Soon, the boy began skipping school and getting into trouble. His association with the group is at least one factor given for his deadly rampage at his school.

But aside from a feeling of belonging, cliques also serve to keep others out. Sociologists Patti and Peter Adler have studied teenage cliques. One clique member told them that "one of the main things to do is to keep picking on unpopular kids because it's just fun to do."[7] And sometimes clique members are thrown out if they are seen socializing with "outsiders." Cliques are generally not seen as dangerous until they cross the line and become cults or gangs.

Cults

On October 1, 1997, upset over the breakup with his girlfriend, a sixteen-year-old student in Pearl, Mississippi, went on a rampage. After stabbing his mother to death, the boy drove to the school with a rifle under his trench coat and killed his former girlfriend and another girl and wounded seven others. Later, six other teens were arrested as accomplices. It was soon discovered that the teens had been involved in a cult alternately called Kroth or "The Group."

Police had found sacrificed animals around bonfire ashes before. Local clergymen said they were not surprised that some teens dabbled in the occult as a way of rebelling against their parents. But the seven-member Kroth group went beyond dabbling. They read and quoted works by Adolf Hitler and nineteenth-century German philosopher Friedrich Nietzsche (who challenged traditional forms of religion and morality). By several accounts, the group had planned a gun and bomb assault on the school. They planned to later carry out an attack on a mall in the nearby city of Jackson.[8]

Professor Paul J. Ciborowski says cults can become dangerous when members begin to adopt negative or extreme ideas and fantasies. Then members reinforce those ideas for each other.[9] Cults can also prod members to prove their allegiance, much the same way that gangs have initiation rites.

Gangs

Gangs tend to be more formal and organized than cliques. There are strict rules and dress codes. The gang requires members to act in certain ways or be excluded. They often have to prove their loyalty to the group.

Part of the attraction of gangs is the sense of caring and belonging many gang members feel. Kenny, a Los Angeles gang leader, says, "A gang, it's like your family. You know, we do for each other. It's better than a family because a family don't always support what you do, but you know your homeboys are with you."[10]

But although gangs may provide a sense of family, members are also more likely to get into trouble with the law, get injured, or even die. Experts at the Justice Department have noted the link between the juvenile murder arrest rate and the use of crack cocaine and the violent gangs that deal in it.[11] When gangs get into battles over "home turf"—certain areas that belong to certain gangs—these disputes can bring about violence in school. And as more and more gangs deal in drugs, profits from sales are often used for buying more deadly weapons. Research confirms that gang members are more likely to bring guns to school.[12]

Now there are "gang prevention" programs designed to reach kids before gangs do. Although there is some evidence that these programs can change students' attitudes toward gangs,[13] it has not yet been determined whether gang membership has actually decreased as a result. Some programs focus on providing job training so gang members can qualify for good jobs rather than participate in illegal activities for income.

Drugs and Alcohol

Numerous studies have shown the strong link between substance use and school violence. Using substances such as marijuana or alcohol in school has been associated with both being a victim of violence and being an aggressor.[14]

Authorities say that drugs and alcohol influence violence in schools in several ways. One way is the violence that erupts when drug deals go wrong. In Dove Creek, Colorado, a high school football player was shot nineteen times. His body was dumped in the Utah desert and was not found for a week. Later it was found that the murder had been over a drug deal. One of the three people arrested was a fellow team member.

There is another way drugs and alcohol can affect teens. Illegal substances can alienate teens from others and lead them to act violently. One study examined the connection between illegal substances and violence in schools. Researchers found that the more drugs were prevalent in a school, the more likely it would be that students carried a weapon, had physical fights, had their property stolen or damaged, and were absent from school because of feeling unsafe.[15]

*G*uns, alcohol, and drugs can be a lethal mix.

When the shooter in Santee, California, started

acting differently, his friends credited a group called the "Grommits" for the change in his behavior. The new friends skipped school and hung out at the local park, smoking marijuana and drinking tequila stolen from the grocery store. A former girlfriend said later, "We would just sit there and smoke weed. Bong loads, pipes, joints, you name it—he smoked it."[16]

Alcohol and drugs can also cause the lowering of inhibitions in people. All human beings have inhibitions—internal controls that keep us from acting out on every single emotion we feel. This may be especially true of angry or violent emotions. We learn to express anger, frustration, or irritation in socially acceptable ways. But when inhibitions are lowered by alcohol or drugs, people are more likely to express strong emotions in physical ways.

Students who admit to using alcohol and drugs at school have higher gun possession rates.[17] They tend to have poorer attendance, worse behavior, lower academic achievement, and higher rates of dropping out of school.

Although the interaction among guns, cults and gangs, and drugs and alcohol is not yet completely understood, one thing is certain. They are all considered risk factors. That is, involvement with weapons, illegal substances, and fringe groups puts teens at risk of being violent. But what can be done to reduce these behaviors in and out of school?

Chapter 5

Controversial Methods

In December 1997, the small town of West Paducah, Kentucky, was thrust into the national spotlight when a fourteen-year-old killed three fellow students and wounded five others at Heath High School. The freshman had simply wrapped up his guns and eight hundred rounds of ammunition in blankets and tape and put them in his backpack. When a teacher questioned him about the large package, he said it was for a science project. The teacher believed him, and the shooter snuck his deadly arsenal into the school.

The legacy of that tragic day is evident today at Heath High School as students, teachers, and visitors must wear identification tags around their necks at all times. Students also line up each morning before entering school to have their bags searched. The school has also required students to sign consent forms allowing the search of their cars for weapons. Staff have been given two-way radios to wear on their belts and emergency medical kits. Disaster-instruction manuals have been placed in every classroom.[1]

In the wake of high-profile school shootings, many schools adopted more security measures. Dozens of companies seemingly emerged overnight, selling everything from training videos and seminars to surveillance cameras and metal detectors. Stores reported an increase in school orders for items such as transparent plastic backpacks.[2] Some schools permanently locked or even removed hall lockers. Imposing fences and automatically locking doors and gates were installed. Other schools issued computerized ID cards or introduced card entry systems for students. And virtually all school districts began issuing stricter rules and tougher punishments for student misbehavior.

But these stricter codes were not always welcomed. Students complained that they were being treated like criminals. Educators disapproved of the prisonlike settings. Parents protested that their parental rights were being taken away. And crime experts pointed out that the juvenile murder rate has been consistently decreasing in recent years and that arrests for violence among teens were the lowest in a decade.[3]

Dress Codes

After the Columbine tragedy, one of the first policies taken by most schools was stricter dress codes. Peers of the Trench Coat Mafia reported that members of the group often came to school wearing ankle-length black coats, steel-toed boots, and Nazi crosses. Schools around the country immediately banned the coats, boots, black fingernail polish, and other apparel associated with "Goth" or "shock rock" groups.

At West Mecklenburg High School in North Carolina, seventeen-year-old Cliff Riggins found himself under suspicion just because of how he dressed. School officials pulled him aside to ask him why he tended to dress and paint his nails in black and why he sometimes wore a black coat. Even though Cliff had never even been in a fistfight, he felt he was being marked as potentially violent. Cliff protested, "Maybe I don't look like everyone else, but it's not like I'm gonna go shoot up the school."[4]

*I*n response to school shootings, some schools have forbidden such clothing as baggy pants.

Many schools prohibit baggy clothing because of its ability to conceal weapons. The teenage shooter at Heritage High School in Conyers, Georgia, was able to sneak in a sawed-off .22-caliber rifle strapped to his leg and a .357-caliber handgun tucked into his baggy pants.

But many students and parents complain about the strict dress codes, saying that they are unfair. And sometimes school administrators have misinterpreted student clothing. In Salt Lake City, Utah, for example, a student was suspended for wearing a T-shirt with the word "vegan" on it. Vegan refers to a strict vegetarian diet. School administrators thought the word referred to a violent local gang and banned the student from campus. And one Pensacola, Florida, high school sophomore received a ten-day suspension for having a nail clipper. Extreme cases like these continue to challenge strict dress code policies.

Technology

A number of technological solutions were proposed soon after the Columbine shootings. Many schools began using metal detectors and X-ray inspections, alarm systems, and video camera surveillance. Telephones and panic buttons were installed in classrooms. Toll-free, anonymous hot lines were created so students could report weapons possession, drug use or drug sales, or threats made by fellow students. And in some schools, students must swipe a card through a computerized system to be able to enter the building.

Even though most security equipment is installed in high schools and middle schools, metal detectors have even made it to elementary schools. After three students brought guns to schools, an Indiana school district became the first in the United States in 1998 to install metal detectors in its elementary schools.

But many people argue that electronic devices invade privacy. Some also argue that the "get-tough" measures often do more harm than good. These stricter policies, they say, can lead to a "lockdown mentality," making schools seem like prisons. Uniformed security guards and undercover police can alienate students, making them suspicious of school personnel. They may also make the school seem like a military camp.

Experts also point out that anonymous tips do not tend to be very reliable. Deborah Ross, executive director of the North Carolina chapter of the American Civil Liberties Union (ACLU), says that hot-line tips are "even less reliable when you're talking about kids, who are more likely to play practical jokes."[5]

Searches

Another security measure taken by schools is the searching of students' bags, lockers, and desks. Although the U.S. Constitution's Fourth Amendment protects citizens from searches without reasonable cause, the protection is not the same in schools. School officials do not need "probable cause" to search students or their possessions. Court cases have established that providing a safe learning environment overrides individual rights. School officials say that the strict measures are necessary in today's world. At West Mecklenburg High School, security officers interrupt classes to conduct surprise searches about once a month.[6]

Critics argue that these stricter policies can encroach on people's rights. Searches of students, their belongings, and their lockers may violate their constitutional rights. Some districts are getting around the legal issues by having students sign consent forms. Vincent Schiraldi, director of the Justice Policy Institute in Washington, D.C., is also coauthor of *School House Hype*. The report dispels many of the myths associated with school violence. Schiraldi says, "We're shredding the Constitution with random locker searches and anonymous hotlines."[7]

Many parents at Heath High School in Kentucky, where a shooting took place in 1997, are not happy about the changes in security. One mother says, "From what I understand, the Constitution is still in effect. I don't like the idea of my child going to school and having school officials search him at their discretion. They're trying their best, but they don't seem to be getting it right."[8]

Heath High's principal Bill Bond defends his school's strict environment. He explains, "We have restrictions on everything we do. I've never thought about carrying a bomb on an airplane, but I pass through airport security just like everybody else. The very concept of security is always going to reduce freedom. That is a trade-off people have been dealing with since the beginning of time."[9]

Drills

Among the many tragic lessons provided by the Columbine shootings was the realization that the police are ill-equipped to respond to school violence. Since then, school districts have staged mock shootings complete with drama students posing as the shooters and as wounded students begging for help, fake pipe bombs, and real helicopters and SWAT teams.[10]

R-U-Ready High School is a training center in North Carolina. SWAT teams and police officers learn how to deal with school shootings and other dangerous situations. By preparing law enforcement officers to respond quickly, it is hoped that the number of deaths and injuries would be decreased during these crises. Some agencies have even equipped patrol cars with computers that can call up school floor plans.

Another strategy is to have mock drills. One school that instituted "lockdown" drills was George E. Round Elementary School in Manassas, Virginia. When students heard the principal's voice on the P.A. announcing "Code A!" they knew to crouch below their desks. Teachers knew to lock their doors, turn out the lights, and pull down the shades. The drill was to simulate how they should respond if a dangerous person with a gun entered the building. Such drills are controversial because they are upsetting to students and teachers, and it is not conclusive whether such drills help improve people's reactions in real emergencies.

Zero Tolerance

Another response has been to adopt stricter school rules and dispense tougher punishment for breaking them. About 90 percent of school districts in the United States have "zero tolerance" policies.[11] The name of the policy refers to authorities showing no mercy if, for example, a student comes to school with a gun—even a toy gun that looks like the real thing. Punishment typically ranges from a few days of suspension to permanent expulsion. In some school districts, students who break a serious rule (such as drug or weapon possession) do not even get a first warning—punishment is swift and automatic.

Police and school officials say they can take no chances and that even *threats* of violence must be taken seriously. A thirteen-year-old boy in New York, for example, was arrested after he posted a "hit list" on his Web page and threatened to plant a bomb in his middle school.[12] Zero tolerance rules are even being applied to students who overheard threats but did not report them.

Violent language has also been targeted by zero tolerance policies. After writing a Halloween story in which he described shooting his teacher and two classmates, a seventh-grader in Ponder, Texas, was held in juvenile detention for five days.[13] Violent language, even if it is intended as a joke, can now get a student expelled.

The policy can backfire, however, and school districts have been strongly criticized for issuing punishments that do not seem to fit the crime. In Sayreville, New Jersey, for example, four kindergarten students were suspended for three days for pointing fingers at each other and pretending to shoot. The principal followed the district's policy strictly, saying, "Given the climate of our society, we cannot take any of these statements in a light manner."[14] Protests by the parents and in the community were immediate. The assistant superintendent staunchly defended the school's action, saying that it was better to be cautious even if "you look like a bunch of fools."[15]

In Tampa, Florida, one father was outraged when his twelve-year-old son, Adam, was arrested for being involved in a false bomb threat. According to the parent, Adam was asked by a classmate for a quarter. The student then placed the bomb threat to their middle school from a phone booth using the quarter Adam had given him. The enraged father protested his son's arrest, saying, "It's guilt by association. Adam was not provided the most basic constitutional rights ... and he was denied the most basic human right, access to his parents, for having committed the heinous [horrible] act of lending a schoolmate a quarter."[16]

Opponents of zero tolerance policies say that school administrators need to consider a student's motive. In

Louisiana, a twelve-year-old said in the cafeteria lunch line, "If you take all the potatoes, I'm gonna get you."[17] Because the remark was interpreted as a threat, the student was suspended from school and spent two weeks in juvenile detention. In rural areas, some students unintentionally break the rules when they drive onto campus in the family pickup truck with a loaded gun rack in the back window.

While school officials sympathize with students who break rules accidentally, they argue that zero tolerance is

Zero Tolerance Policies

Zero tolerance policies are defined as school or district rules that mandate predetermined consequences or punishments for specific offenses. Punishments usually include out-of-school suspension, expulsion, or transfer to an alternative school or program.

Percentage of Public Schools That Have Adopted Zero Tolerance Policies for Specific Offenses: 1996-97

Type of Offense	Percentage
Alcohol	87
Drugs	88
Firearms	94
Tobacco	79
Violence	79
Weapons other than firearms	91

Source: U.S. Department of Education, National Center for Education Statistics, Fast Response Survey System, "Principal/School Disciplinarian Survey on School Violence," FRSS 63, 1997.

necessary. One assistant superintendent points out, "A weapon brought by a student, even without the intent to do harm, often ends up doing harm anyway."[18] Paul Houston, the executive director of the American Association of School Administrators, calls it "the Columbine effect." Houston explains, "An administrator can no longer afford to ignore potential threats even if it looks like it is not serious."[19] In some districts, scissors, pocket knives, and even nail clippers can land a student a suspension from school. Some of the more extreme cases have prompted one ACLU director to decry "subzero tolerance." He says, "Subzero tolerance is where punishment is given for behavior that doesn't even violate any rules."[20]

To ward off critics, some districts with zero tolerance policies have also adopted "diversion programs." First-time offenders may be given a second chance if they write letters of apology, do community service, and receive counseling. If they complete the program, students do not get a criminal record. Diversion programs have critics, however. They point out that the two Columbine killers paid weekly visits to a "diversion officer" and were ordered to participate in a number of reform programs (they had previously been arrested for stealing electronic equipment). The program officers for both boys had marked their prognosis as "good."[21]

Profiling

Perhaps the most controversial method has been developing "profiles" of potentially violent teens. The practice involves identifying students who exhibit behaviors associated with violence, such as being alienated, being bullied, or hurting animals. If potentially violent teens can be reached before they strike out, so the argument goes, the incidence of violence will decrease. There is even a computer program, Mosaic 2000, that claims to identify troubled teens before they act out violently. By using such risk factors as "alarming" talk, certain kinds of clothing,

A security officer adjusts the controls on a monitor showing several locations in a high school. Many school systems are using video surveillance systems in the wake of Columbine and other school shootings.

access to guns, and the abuse of animals, school officials using the program can pinpoint students who are potentially violent. The makers of Mosaic say that the system does *not* profile students, but actually helps school officials look beyond a student's outward image. One of the developers of the program says, "It's easy to pick out the gang members with tattoos. It's these other people that kind of surprise administrators, and these are the ones they really need to identify."[22]

Nonetheless, there are several problems with using profiling. The biggest issue is the possibility of predicting a student to be violent, and having that prediction turn out to be false. As one police officer points out, "A kid dyes his hair purple and dresses in black—that may be strange to you or me, but it doesn't mean he's going to go out and kill someone."[23]

Profiling can also suffer from the opposite problem: not identifying students who are likely to act out violently. When middle school teacher Barry Grunow was shot and killed by one of his students on the last day of school, the community was shocked enough by the senseless act of violence. What was even more surprising was that the killer was a "good kid" who got mostly As and Bs and was described as having a cheerful personality. Teachers and peers were so impressed by his maturity that he had been nominated to be a peer mediator to help other kids resolve conflicts.[24] By most profiling checklists, he would not be identified as a potential school shooter.

Another problem with profiling students is civil liberties violations. Critics argue that the use of programs such as Mosaic invades students' privacy. After a potentially violent student is identified, it is likely that the student would have to be monitored, restricted, or even confined. Barry Steinhardt, associate director of the ACLU, says, "These programs treat children as suspects, not students."[25] In 1975, the United States Supreme Court ruled in *Goss* v. *Lopez* that all students have a right to a warning and hearing before they are suspended or expelled.

Groups such as the Federal Bureau of Investigation and the Secret Service have both rejected profiling as an effective way of combating school violence. In a study on violent students published by the FBI, the organization opposed the practice of profiling, saying that it was virtually impossible to predict which students are likely to commit a violent act.[26] The Secret Service's National Threat Assessment Center examined forty recent school shootings and interviewed some of the shooters. The Center concluded, "There's no one set of characteristics that describes a school shooter."[27]

Legislation

School safety has been at the center of several federal programs and legislative efforts. When the National

Education Goals Panel set forth their plan to improve American schools, they included a safe environment. Goal Seven of the National Education Goals specifically promotes school safety: "Every school in the United States will be free of drugs, violence, and unauthorized presence of firearms and alcohol and will offer a disciplined environment conducive to learning."[28]

Some measures are worded more strictly. The federal Gun-Free Schools Act, passed in 1994, virtually ensures expulsion for any student found with a gun at school. The law requires school districts to specify the consequences of threatening others, using drugs or alcohol on campus, and possessing weapons.

Many school districts have also passed antiharassment policies designed to eliminate bullying. The Washington State senate, for example, passed a law that requires school officials to investigate any bullying incident on campus. The law also requires schools to inform parents about bullying. Under these rules, students could receive counseling or punishment for name-calling, teasing, or making fun of other students' appearance.

However, these policies are being challenged in court by people who feel that the rules violate their right to free speech. In Pennsylvania, for example, a suit was filed on behalf of two students whose religion teaches that homosexuality is a sin. They claim that the school board's antiharassment policy interferes with their First Amendment rights. The matter is still being settled by the courts.[29]

In Massachusetts, teachers will be allowed to restrain unruly students who pose a danger to themselves or others. Previously, teachers were not allowed to hold down students. The education commissioner said, "We hope restraints won't be used often anyway, but we have to have something for the safety of the faculty and students."[30]

Proposition 21, a law passed in California, calls for treating juveniles fourteen and older who commit serious crimes as adults. Under the tough law, young offenders are tried in adult court, where punishments are harsher. California is also taking the lead on the controversial practice of having bullies visit a morgue and watch autopsies. The Los Angeles board of supervisors for schools proposed the shock treatment to show students the effects of gunshot wounds, stabbings, and the reality of death. The measure had already been imposed on teens who were caught drinking and driving. Now, bullies and students who make violent threats will also be required to attend an autopsy as part of their "treatment." Critics argue, however, that "it is a superficial approach and doesn't deal with the real issues."[31]

School: A Toxic Environment?

These controversial measures have led some critics to charge that "the schoolhouse [has become] toxic for too many children."[32] Experts fear that in these anxious environments, learning may be hampered. Educational psychologist Renate Nummela Caine believes that when students feel endangered or vulnerable, their ability to think becomes limited and their creativity becomes severely inhibited. Caine says, "What schools are doing is creating conditions that are comparable to prisons. Where else are people searched every day and watched every minute?"[33]

In light of these accusations, administrators are trying hard to create school climates that are warm and receptive. Educators are experimenting with new programs that promise to improve students' attitudes and behavior. And communities are working together with law enforcement agencies to stem juvenile violence. The question remains: What kinds of programs have been most effective?

Chapter 6

Effective Responses from Schools and Communities

Educators, parents, and others in the community are actively searching for ways to stem and prevent school violence. As Joe Schneider of the American Association of School Administrators says, "Everyone feels the need to do something, even though no one agrees on what that should be."[1]

Most schools have already beefed up security by employing security guards, installing surveillance cameras, and using metal detectors. Unfortunately, most of the intervention strategies used by schools are employed after a student has already exhibited problem behaviors. Experts warn that some strategies are ineffective and may even be dangerous. For example, one marketer is skeptical about the usefulness of see-through backpacks. He says, "I'm afraid it will give false security to the schools. I think someone can stick a knife or a gun in between two books."[2]

Most experts conclude that because the problem of school violence is a complex one, "piecemeal, isolated efforts to prevent violence are doomed to fail."[3] Schools, parents, students, and the community need to collaborate to identify the causes of violence and find ways to address them.

Opening Lines of Communication

After a fifteen-year-old boy killed two fellow students and wounded thirteen other people at Santana High School in California, four of his peers and an adult came forward to say that he had made violent threats the previous weekend. But his friends thought the boy was joking and no one warned the authorities. Fearing for the four students' safety after they received threats, officials barred them from campus for the remainder of the school year. One of the students said, "I do regret that I didn't do something. That's going to be with me for a long time."[4]

Students need to feel comfortable in reporting potential violence in their schools. One aspect of the Littleton tragedy that shocked many people is that although the students knew all about the Trench Coat Mafia, most parents had never heard of the outcast group. Neither the school's faculty nor its principal knew about the group. Students seem to have an informal code of silence regarding their peers. In a study of recent school shootings conducted by the Secret Service, it was found that although the shooters had not necessarily told adults about their intentions, they had recorded plans in diaries, Web sites, and had told several other kids.[5]

The chief of school security in Alachua County, Florida, says, "Students are the first line of defense. They're the people who know what's going down."[6] So many schools are now focusing on getting students to feel more responsible for their school's safety and less hesitant about reporting problems. Ronald Stephens of the National School Safety Center says, "The best metal detector is the student."[7]

But many students are afraid of being called tattletales if they report problems. Bruce T. Blythe, president of a crisis management company, insists that student comfort in reporting suspicious behavior is key. He says the message needs to be repeated to overcome students' resistance to telling on friends.[8] Students need to know that telling about potential violence is not tattling.

Before a thirteen-year-old student in Lake Worth, Florida, shot and killed his teacher, Barry Grunow, in May 2000, he had shown the handgun he used to at least two other students. No adult was told. After the shooting, the school district adopted a new approach, a thirteen-week program called "Silence Hurts." The Silence Hurts campaign is based on national research and a report by the Secret Service that found that in 75 percent of school shootings, other students had known about the planned attack. The purpose of the program is to stress to students the importance of keeping adults informed of what is going on with their peers.[9]

Some communities are honoring students who have prevented possible tragedies by telling a trusted adult. Seventeen-year-old Victoria Sudd told her mother she had overheard two boys on the school bus talk about killing people. When police searched the boys' homes, they found a rifle and a "hit list" of students. The city of Twentynine Palms, California, where Victoria lives, plans to give her an award for her actions.[10]

Recognizing Warning Signs

Most experts agree that the key in preventing crises is to be able to recognize early warning signs. Teachers, students, administrators, and school support staff all need to be alert to hints that a youth is troubled.

The Columbine Review Commission set up by Colorado's governor concluded that the killers had actually "practiced" for their rampage. The two teenagers had made videotapes, had created a Web site, and had even written a school essay about their intentions.[11]

Violent language is one trait found in common among many of the school shooters. The fourteen-year-old who opened fire at his middle school in Washington in 1996 had told a friend how cool it would be to go on a shooting spree. The seventeen-year-old who killed his parents and two students at Thurston High School in Springfield, Oregon, frequently spoke of shooting cats, blowing up cows, and making bombs.

Experts warn, however, that using violent language is not always a good predictor of violent behavior. Kevin Dwyer, president of the National Association of School Psychologists says, "These things may be indicators, and they may not. To try to predict an individual's future behavior based on what they say or write isn't really possible."[12]

Programs for Students

When trying to eliminate school violence, one of the likeliest places to start is with the students themselves. Just as it can be learned, violent behavior can be unlearned. The Justice Policy Institute recommends that to prevent the problem in the first place, counseling and antiviolence programs for kids may be the most effective means. Some research has found that students who are involved in their schoolwork, who feel bonded to their school, and who have lots of opportunities to participate and succeed are less likely to commit violence.[13]

Many schools are now focusing on teaching students nonviolent ways to solve problems and conflicts. One school supervisor says, "When a child is displaying antisocial behaviors, you can't just say 'Stop.' You also have to teach them prosocial skills."[14] Popular approaches include anger management training for students and conflict resolution programs. In peer mediation programs, students volunteer for training. Then they act as negotiators and help fellow students solve their conflicts. Some students also volunteer to be peer counselors. They listen and help students who are angry, depressed, or alienated.

Some schools are also adopting the Take a Stand Program, which teaches kids how to reduce bullying at their school. Sherryll Kraizer, executive director of the Denver-based Coalition for Children, says that the key is to start early in elementary school. Kraizer says, "Just like the cultural shift in wearing seat belts came from

Warning Signs

After studying common characteristics of youngsters who have caused school-associated violent deaths, the National School Safety Center has identified the following behaviors, which could indicate a youth's potential for harming him/herself or others:

- Has a history of tantrums and uncontrollable angry outbursts.
- Characteristically resorts to name calling, cursing, or abusive language.
- Habitually makes violent threats when angry.
- Has previously brought a weapon to school.
- Has a background of serious disciplinary problems at school and in the community.
- Has a background of drug, alcohol, or other substance abuse or dependency.
- Is on the fringe of his/her peer group with few or no close friends.
- Is preoccupied with weapons, explosives, or other incendiary devices.
- Has previously been truant, suspended, or expelled from school.
- Displays cruelty to animals.
- Has little or no supervision and support from parents or a caring adult.
- Has witnessed or been a victim of abuse or neglect in the home.
- Has been bullied and/or bullies or intimidates peers or younger children.
- Tends to blame others for difficulties and problems she/he causes her/himself.
- Consistently prefers TV shows, movies, or music expressing violent themes and acts.
- Prefers reading materials dealing with violent themes, rituals, and abuse.
- Reflects anger, frustration, and the dark side of life in school essays or writing projects.
- Is involved with a gang or an antisocial group on the fringe of peer acceptance.
- Is often depressed and/or has significant mood swings.
- Has threatened or attempted suicide.

Source: "Checklist of Characteristics of Youth Who Have Caused School-Associated Violent Deaths," *National School Safety Center Page*, 1998, <http://www. nsscl.org/reporter/checklist.htm> (September 6, 2001).

elementary school kids; children can say we're not going to treat each other this way."[15]

It is the power of negative groups (such as gangs) that some programs try to replace. One successful approach has been Positive Peer Groups (PPG) in Ohio. Since 1990 PPG has helped alienated students develop positive attitudes toward school and society. The program offers leadership training and opportunities for group activities. It is introduced at the middle school level and takes twenty-five weeks. Typically, students are asked to identify a school or community problem. Then they propose and work together to achieve a solution. The results have been impressive. Most of the participants have shown an improved attitude toward their teachers, peers, and community.[16]

There is also the national Hands Project. Symbolized by a purple hand, this violence prevention program teaches people that while "anger is a feeling, violence is a choice." Schools and public organizations in forty states have adopted the program. In schools, students are encouraged to say the program pledge daily, at the start of the day. The pledge is: "I will not use my hands or my words for hurting myself or others."[17]

Schools are holding rallies and asking students to sign no-violence pledges. At Sickles Senior High in Tampa, Florida, students are organizing the rallies. As part of the larger "Not in My School" program, students banded together to put a stop to rumors, false bomb threats, and violence.

Many teachers and parents are supporting educational programs such as moral education and character education. These courses give students the opportunity to develop positive values and discuss what it means to be a good citizen. John Leanes, a middle school principal, says, "If we want a kinder, gentler society, we've got to make character education and values as big a part of education as reading, math and science."[18]

One innovative way to curb teen violence is through a poetry curriculum being tried in several schools around the nation. The program is based on research that has found a connection between aggression and a lack of verbal expression. Once kids develop an emotional vocabulary and are given an outlet for that expression, they are less likely to express their anger and frustration through violence. "Slam" poetry combines poetry and performance art. Both the content and the dramatic delivery are highly prized. Slam sessions have been described as "an Olympics of poetry." Slam poetry naturally appeals to many teens since it is heavily influenced by hip-hop and rap. Teachers who have used the method enthusiastically report how writing helps teens release their feelings. And when they perform their piece they receive support and appreciation from their peers. This in turn translates into more tolerance and respect for each other and for their teachers.[19]

Another strategy being used in English and social studies classrooms is to study the life and work of peaceful

*A*t a memorial service, a participant holds an anti-gun sign. Many people have demonstrated against violence in schools and against the availability of guns.

figures in history such as Mahatma Gandhi and Martin Luther King, Jr. By exploring nonviolent means of protest, students become aware that there are alternatives to violence. After employing such a curriculum, schools have reported less fighting among students.[20]

Building Connections

Schools are looking for ways to build connections among students and strengthen their relationship with the home. Educators know that involving parents results in student success. Parent involvement leads to higher attendance rates, lower suspension rates, and better academic achievement.[21] Parents are encouraged to volunteer, join the Parent-Teacher Association, and share their points of view with administrators.

Another way to build connections is to have smaller schools so that students have a sense of belonging. The larger the school, the greater the chance of feeling isolated. In general, students are less likely to misbehave in schools where they are known. James Garbarino says, "If I could do one single thing [to reduce teen violence], it would be to ensure that teenagers are not in high schools bigger than 400 to 500 students."[22]

Professor Kathleen Heide, who has studied juvenile criminals for more than twenty years, says she is "concerned but not pessimistic."[23] Heide's research and that of others has led her to conclude that often having just one person in a child's life who takes an active interest in him or her can make all the difference. That person does not necessarily have to be a parent—sometimes a grandparent, a coach, or a teacher can be just as important.

Educators, parents, students, and ordinary citizens hope that by improving the school climate and developing close relationships with kids, the nightmare of school violence will stop. Although every school shooting has been a tragedy, it has also provided lessons. Let us hope that these lessons will lead the way to safer and better schools in the future.

1978—*February 22*: In Lansing, Michigan, a fifteen-year-old high school student shoots and kills one classmate and wounds another at Everett High School.

May 19: In Austin, Texas, a thirteen-year-old honor student shoots his teacher to death.

1985—*January 21*: In Goddard, Kansas, a fourteen-year-old kills the principal and three others at his junior high school.

1986—*December 4*: In Lewistown, Montana, after failing French, a fourteen-year-old student tries to kill his teacher but shoots and kills her substitute instead. He also injures a vice principal and two students.

1988—*December 16*: In Virginia Beach, Virginia, at his private Christian school, a sixteen-year-old kills one teacher, wounds an assistant principal, and fires upon a student who had called him a racist name.

1993—*January 18*: In Grayson, Kentucky, a seventeen-year-old holds his high school English class hostage after shooting and killing his teacher and a custodian.

1995—*October 12*: Blackville, South Carolina, after being suspended for making an obscene gesture, a sixteen-year-old shoots two teachers, wounding one and killing the other. He then shoots and kills himself.

November 15: In Lynnville, Tennessee, a seventeen-year-old shoots and critically wounds one teacher, then kills another teacher and a fellow student at Richland School.

1996—*February 2*: In Moses Lake, Washington, a fourteen-year-old junior high school student sneaks a rifle into school and kills two students and a teacher and wounds another student in his algebra class.

September 25: In Scottsdale, Georgia, a sixteen-year-old student at the DeKalb Alternative School shoots and kills his teacher.

October 31: In St. Louis, Missouri, a sixteen-year-old shoots and critically wounds a fellow student in a hallway of Sumner High School. The student dies the following day after surgery.

1997—*February 19*: In Bethel, Alaska, a sixteen-year-old boy kills his school's principal and a student and injures two others.

October 1: In Pearl, Mississippi, a sixteen-year-old kills his mother, and goes to his high school and opens fire, killing two students and wounding seven others.

December 1: In West Paducah, Kentucky, a fourteen-year-old kills three fellow students and wounds five others at Heath High School.

December 15: In Stamps, Arkansas, while hiding in nearby woods, a fourteen-year-old shoots and wounds two students as they stand in the school parking lot.

1998—*March 24*: In Jonesboro, Arkansas, two boys, eleven and thirteen years old, open fire on their middle school from nearby woods, killing four girls and a teacher and wounding ten others.

April 24: In Edinboro, Pennsylvania, a fourteen-year-old kills his science teacher and wounds two students at an eighth-grade dance.

May 19: In Fayetteville, Tennessee, three days before graduation, an eighteen-year-old honor student kills a classmate who is dating his ex-girlfriend.

May 21: In Springfield, Oregon, after killing his parents, a seventeen-year-old opens fire in Thurston High School, killing two students and wounding twenty others.

1999—*April 20*: In Littleton, Colorado, two high school students kill twelve students and a teacher and wound another 23 before committing suicide.

May 20: In Conyers, Georgia, a fifteen-year-old wounds six of his classmates at Heritage High School.

November 19: In Deming, New Mexico, a twelve-year-old boy shoots a thirteen-year-old girl in the head in the lobby of their middle school; she dies the following day.

December 6: In Fort Gibson, Oklahoma, a seventh-grade boy fires into a crowd waiting outside his middle school, wounding five students.

2000—*February 29*: In Mount Morris Township, Michigan, following a playground dispute the day before, a six-year-old boy shoots and kills a female classmate in their first-grade classroom.

May 26: In Lake Worth, Florida, after being sent home for playing with water balloons, a thirteen-year-old boy shoots and kills his middle school teacher.

2001—*March 5*: In Santee, California, after threatening to take a gun to school, a fifteen-year-old boy kills two fellow students and wounds thirteen people at his high school.

March 6: In Williamsport, Pennsylvania, bringing a gun to school, a fourteen-year-old girl wounds a fellow eighth-grade girl in the shoulder at their private Catholic school. The case is unusual in that the shooter is female.

March 22: In El Cajon, California, after he wounds three students and a teacher at Granite Hills High School, an eighteen-year-old enters into a gun battle with a school security officer.

Center for the Prevention of School Violence
313 Chapanoke Road, Suite 140
Raleigh, North Carolina 27603
(800) 299-6054

Justice Policy Institute
1234 Massachusetts Ave, NW, Suite C1009
Washington, DC 20005
(202) 737-7270

National Crime Prevention Council
1000 Connecticut Avenue, NW, 13th Floor
Washington, DC 20036
(202) 466-6272

National Resource Center for Safe Schools
101 SW Main, Suite 500
Portland, OR 97204
(800) 268-2275

National School Safety Center
141 Duesenberg Drive, Suite 11
Westlake Village, CA 91362
(805) 373-9977

Safe Communities, Safe Schools
Institute of Behavioral Science
University of Colorado at Boulder, 439 UCB
Boulder, CO 80309-0439
(303) 492-8465

For More Information

Chapter 1. A Growing Concern

1. "Colorado Killers Inspired Youth In Georgia Shooting, Note Says," *The New York Times*, August 10, 1999, p. A10.

2. Sally Roberts and Roberto Ceniceros, "Preventing Another School Tragedy," *Business Insurance*, April 26, 1999, p. 1.

3. Robin McDowell, "16 Dead in Colorado School Shooting," *The Denver Post*, April 21, 1999, p. A1.

4. Melody M. Yarbrough and Nestor W. Sherman, "Predictors of Violent Behavior in Youth," *Research Quarterly for Exercise and Sport*, vol. 71, March 2000, p. 47.

5. Callie M. Rennison, *Criminal Victimization* 1998 (Washington, D.C.: U.S. Department of Justice, 1999), p. 6.

6. U.S. Department of Justice and U.S. Department of Education, *Annual Report on School Safety* (Washington, D.C.: 1999).

7. Mindy Sink, "Shootings Intensify Interest in Home Schooling," *The New York Times*, August 11, 1999, p. B7.

8. Ibid.

9. Joe Agron and Larry Anderson, "School Security by the Numbers," *American School & University*, vol. 72, May 2000, p. C6.

10. Sink, p. B7.

Chapter 2. The Nagging Question: Why?

1. "Study: Cutting TV Time Trims Kids' Aggression," *St. Petersburg Times*, January 15, 2001, p. 5A.

2. National School Safety Center, "Checklist of Characteristics of Youth Who Have Caused School-Associated Violent Deaths," 1998, <http://www.nssc1.org/reporter/checklist.htm> (August 19, 2001).

3. John Martin Rich, "Predicting and Controlling School Violence," *Contemporary Education*, Fall 1992, p. 36.

4. Associated Press, "U.S. Students Have Easy Access to Guns, Survey Finds," *CNNfyi.com Education News*, April 2, 2001, <http://fyi.cnn.com/2001/fyi/teachers.ednews/04/02/gun.access.ap/index.html> (August 17, 2001).

5. Dorothy L. Espelage et al., "Examining the Social Context of Bullying Behaviors in Early Adolescence," *Journal of Counseling & Development*, vol. 78, Summer 2000, pp. 326–333.

6. Karen S. Peterson, "Parents Restored to Primary Place in Child Development," *USA Today*, August 4, 1999, p. 8D.

7. Ibid.

8. Philip J. Cook et al., "The Medical Costs of Gunshot Injuries in the United States," *The Journal of the American Medical Association*, vol. 282, 1999, p. 447.

9. Carl Levin, "Violence in Our Society," *Congressional Record*, vol. 145, May 6, 1999, p. S4839.

10. Associated Press, "U.S. Students Have Easy Access to Guns, Survey Finds," *CNNfyi.com Education News*, April 2, 2001, <http://fyi.cnn.com/2001/fyi/teachers.ednews/04/02/gun.access.ap/index.html> (August 17, 2001).

11. George Gordon, "Kayla Had Everything Dedric Wanted, So He Shot Her," *The Sunday Telegraph*, March 5, 2000, p. 21.

12. Mike Males, "The Shadow of Poverty in America," *In These Times*, vol. 24, June 12, 2000, pp. 24–25.

13. "Dark Heart of Small Town America," *The Observer*, March 5, 2000, p. 21.

14. Espelage et al., p. 326.

15. Ron Banks, *Bullying in Schools* (Champaign, Ill.: ERIC Clearinghouse on Elementary and Early Childhood Education, 1997), p. 1.

16. U.S. Department of Education, *Indicators of School Crime and Safety* (Washington, D.C. : U.S. DOE, 1999), p. 11.

17. Dorothy Espelage and Barbara Sandler, "Schoolroom Torment," *People*, February 5, 2001, p. 91.

18. Brian Vossekuil et al., *Safe School Initiative* (Washington, D.C.: U.S. Secret Service National Threat Assessment Center, 2000), p. 7.

19. Harriet Barovick et al., "A Curse of Cliques," *Time*, May 3, 1999, p. 44.

20. Banks, p. 2.

21. Terry McCarthy, "Warning," *Time*, March 19, 2001, p. 26.

22. Robin McDowell, Associated Press, "Colorado Suspects Called Outcasts," April 20, 1999.

23. Barovick et al.

24. David Crary, "Secret Service Takes a Crack at Thwarting School Violence," *Tampa Tribune*, August 18, 2000, p. 4.

25. Robert Sullivan, "What Makes a Child Resilient?" *Time*, March 19, 2001, p. 35.

26. Michael Furlong and Gale Morrison, "The School in School Violence: Definitions and Facts," *Journal of Emotional and Behavioral Disorders*, Summer 2000, p. 71.

27. Ibid.

28. Jeanne Weiler, *Girls and Violence* (New York: ERIC Clearinghouse on Urban Education, 1999), p. 1.

29. "Girl Shoots Fellow Eighth Grader," *St. Petersburg Times*, March 8, 2001, p. 3A.

30. "Study: Cutting TV Time Trims Kids' Aggression."

Chapter 3: The Media: Friend or Foe?

1. Keith Naughton and Evan Thomas, "Did Kayla Have to Die?" *Newsweek*, March 13, 2000, p. 24.

2. Kieran Nicholson, "School Killers Put Out Signals," *The Denver Post*, October 28, 2000, p. B1.

3. "Study: Cutting TV Time Trims Kids' Aggression," *St. Petersburg Times*, January 15, 2001, p. 1A.

4. Ibid.

5. John Leland et al., "The Secret Life of Teens," *Newsweek*, May 10, 1999, p. 44.

6. John Martin Rich, "Predicting and Controlling School Violence," *Contemporary Education*, Fall 1992, p. 39.

7. Mike Williams, "Movie 'Factor' in School Shootings," *The Atlanta Journal and Constitution*, December 5, 1997, p. 3A.

8. "Study: Cutting TV Time Trims Kids' Aggression."

9. John Cloud, "The Legacy of Columbine," *Time*, March 19, 2001, p. 33.

10. Pauline B. Gough, "Detoxifying Schools," *Phi Delta Kappan*, March 2000, p. 482.

11. Associated Press, "Juvenile Murder Arrest Rate Is Down," *St. Louis Post-Dispatch*, December 15, 2000, p. A11.

12. U.S. Department of Education, *Annual Report on School Safety* (Washington, D.C.: U.S. DOE, 1999), p. 2.

13. Joe Agron and Larry Anderson, "School Security by the Numbers," *American School & University*, May 2000, p. C6.

14. Vincent Schiraldi, "News Release," Justice Policy Institute, 1999, <http://www.cjcj.org/jpi/schoolhousepr.html> (March 21, 2001).

15. Williams.

16. Maggie Cutler, "Whodunit—the Media?" *The Nation*, March 26, 2001, p. 19.

17. Michael D. Simpson, "After the Shootings, the Lawsuits," *NEA Today*, February 2000, p. 18.

18. Craig Anderson and Karen Dill, "Personality Processes and Individual Differences—Video Games and Aggressive Thoughts, Feelings, and Behavior in the Laboratory and in Life," *Journal of Personality and Social Psychology*, vol. 79, April 2000, p. 772.

19. Elisa Hae-Jung Song and Jane E. Anderson, "How Violent Video Games May Violate Children's Health," *Contemporary Pediatrics*, vol. 18, May 2001, p. 102.

20. Frank D. Roylance, "Internet Gives Youths Path to Hate Groups," *The Baltimore Sun*, April 22, 1999, p. 11A.

21. Jennifer Farrell, "Trashing Jaclyn," *St. Petersburg Times*, March 8, 2001, p. 4D.

22. Aidin Vaziri, "Pop 'Antichrist' Takes Some Time To Reflect," *San Francisco Chronicle*, November 19, 2000, p. 45.

23. Bill Locey, "Out and About," *Los Angeles Times*, September 15, 2000, p. 6B.

24. Edna Gunderson, "Manson Says His Hands Are Clean," *Chicago Sun-Times*, December 2, 2000, p. 33.

25. Charisse Jones, "Rap's Bad Rep," *Los Angeles Times*, May 2, 1993, p. E1.

26. Cutler, p. 19.

27. Walter Isaacson, "Covering the Violence," *Time*, May 31, 1999, p. 6.

Chapter 4. Gangs, Cults, Drugs, and Alcohol

1. Bill Hutchinson, "Well-Planned and Well-Armed, Two Gunmen Had Many Faces," *Daily News*, April 22, 1999, p. 2.

2. Daya Singh Sandhu, "Alienated students: Counseling strategies to curb school violence," *Professional School Counseling*, December 2000, pp. 81–85.

3. Associated Press, "U.S. Students Have Easy Access to Guns, Survey Finds," *CNNfyi.com Education News*, April 2, 2001, <http://fyi.cnn.com/2001/fyi/teachers.ednews/04/02/gun.access.ap/index.html> (August 17, 2001).

4. Judith R. Harris, *The Nurture Assumption: Why Children Turn Out the Way They Do* (New York: Simon & Schuster, 1998).

5. Jerry Adler et al., "The Truth About High School," *Newsweek*, May 10, 1999, p. 56.

6. Terry McCarthy, "Warning," *Time*, March 19, 2001, p. 26.

7. Adam Cohen et al., "A Curse of Cliques," *Time*, May 3, 1999, p. 44.

8. Howard Pankratz, "Columbine Eerily Like Miss. Attack," *The Denver Post*, June 18, 1999, p. A25.

9. Renate Robey, "Danger Lies in Crossing Over to Cults, Experts Say," *The Denver Post*, April 25, 1999, p. 3A.

10. Sally Ann Stewart and Laurel Adams, "Gangs—'It's Like Your Family,'" *USA Today*, December 7, 1989, p. 6A.

11. Associated Press, "Juvenile Murder Arrest Rate Is Down," *St. Louis Post-Dispatch*, December 15, 2000, p. A11.

12. Michael Furlong and Gale Morrison, "The School in School Violence: Definitions and Facts," *Journal of Emotional and Behavioral Disorders*, Summer 2000, p. 71.

13. Quint C. Thurman et al., "Community-Based Gang Prevention and Intervention," *Crime and Delinquency*, vol. 42, April 1996, pp. 279–295.

14. Michael J. Furlong et al., "Drugs and School Violence," *Education and Treatment of Children*, August 1997, pp. 263–280.

15. Richard Lowry et al., "School Violence, Substance Use, and Availability of Illegal Drugs on School Property Among US High School Students," *The Journal of School Health*, November 1999, pp. 347–355.

16. McCarthy, p. 26.

17. Furlong and Morrison, p. 71.

Chapter 5: Controversial Methods

1. Michael Easterbrook, "Taking Aim at Violence," *Psychology Today*, July/August 1999, pp. 52–56.

2. Joshua Harris Prager, "Safety: Back-To-School Sale," *Wall Street Journal*, July 12, 1999, p. A17.

3. Howard N. Snyder and Melissa Sickmund, *Juvenile Offenders and Victims: 1999 National Report* (Washington, D.C.: Office of Juvenile Justice and Delinquency Prevention, 1999), p. 55.

4. Jane Spencer, "Caught in the WAVE," *The Nation*, December 4, 2000, p. 22.

5. Ibid.

6. Ibid.

7. Ibid.

8. Easterbrook, pp. 52–56.

9. Ibid.

10. David Firestone, "After Shootings, Nation's Schools Add to Security," *The New York Times*, August 13, 1999, p. 1.

11. "Schools rethink 'zero tolerance' threats policy," *St. Petersburg Times*, May 17, 2001, p. 3A.

12. Oscar Corral and Joie Tyrrell, "Web Threat Cited in Arrest," *Newsday*, March 22, 2001, p. 5A.

13. Michael D. Simpson, "After the Shootings, the Lawsuits," *NEA Today*, February 2000, p. 18.

14. "Children's Game Nothing to Kid About," *Atlanta Journal and Constitution*, April 6, 2000, p. 1A.

15. Debra Galant, "Bang! You're Suspended," *The New York Times*, April 16, 2000, p. 1NJ.

16. Logan D. Mabe, "Policy on Bomb Threats Thrashed," *St. Petersburg Times*, March 14, 2001, p. 7B.

17. Wendy Kaminer, "The War on High Schools," *The American Prospect*, December 20, 1999, p. 11.

18. Kate Beem, "Schools Face 'Zero Tolerance' Issues," *Kansas City Star*, February 29, 2000, A1.

19. David Karp, "Parents Defend Bomb Chitchat," *St. Petersburg Times*, March 30, 2001, p. 9B.

20. Ethan Bronner, "The clampdown on teen rights," *The New York Times Upfront*, September 6, 1999, pp. 10-14.

21. Daniel Glick, "Anatomy of a Massacre," *Newsweek*, May 3, 1999, p. 24.

22. "Predicting Violence," *The Futurist*, May/June 2000, p. 7.

23. John Elvin, "And Now, Back to School," *Insight on the News*, September 18, 2000, p. 34.

24. Bill Hewitt, "Before the Bell," *People*, June 12, 2000, p. 124.

25. Jodie Morse, "Looking For Trouble," *Time*, April 24, 2000, p. 50.

26. David A. Vise, Kenneth J. Cooper, "FBI Opposes The Profiling of Students," *Techniques*, November 2000, p. 12.

27. Brian Vossekuil et al., *Safe School Initiative* (Washington, D.C.: U.S. Secret Service National Threat Assessment Center, 2000), p. 5.

28. National Education Goals Panel, "Goal 7," *National Education Goals*, n.d., <www.negp.gov/page3-15.htm> (March 2, 2001).

29. Kate Zernike, "Free-Speech Ruling Voids School District's Harassment Policy," *The New York Times*, February 16, 2001, p. A10.

30. "Mass. Teachers Can Restrain Students," *St. Petersburg Times*, February 28, 2001, p. 3A.

31. "School Bully? To the Coroner You Go," The Straits *Times*, March 17, 2001, p. 3.

32. Irwin Hyman and Pamela Snook, "Dangerous Schools and What You Can Do About Them," *Phi Delta Kappan*, March 2000, p. 488.

33. Easterbrook, pp. 52–56.

Chapter 6: Effective Responses from Schools and Communities

1. David Firestone, "After Shootings, Nation's Schools Add to Security," *The New York Times*, August 13, 1999, p. 1A.

2. Joshua Harris Prager, "Safety: Back-To-School Sale," *Wall Street Journal*, July 12, 1999, p. A17.

3. Middle School Partnership, "Student Behavior: Violence in Schools," n.d., <http://www.middleschool.com/studentbehavior/sb_violence.html> (April 5, 2001).

4. "Teen Kills 2, Hurts 13 in School Shooting," *St. Petersburg Times*, March 6, 2001, p. 10A.

5. Bryan Vossekuil et al., *Safe School Initiative* (Washington, D.C.: U.S. Secret Service National Threat Assessment Center, 2000), p. 4.

6. "Campaign Trains Students to Report Rumors," *St. Petersburg Times*, March 9, 2001, p. 4A.

7. John Cloud, "The Legacy of Columbine," *Time*, March 19, 2001, p. 33.

8. Sally Roberts and Roberto Ceniceros, "Preventing Another School Tragedy," *Business Insurance*, April 26, 1999, p. 1.

9. "Teacher's Memory Lives On at Summit on School Safety," *The Tampa Tribune*, August 8, 2000, p. 4.

10. Cloud, p. 33.

11. Kieran Nicholson, "School Killers Put Out Signals," *The Denver Post*, October 28, 2000, p. B1.

12. Michael Easterbrook, "Taking Aim at Violence," *Psychology Today*, July/August 1999, pp. 52–56.

13. Michael Furlong and Gale Morrison, "The School in School Violence: Definitions and Facts," *Journal of Emotional and Behavioral Disorders*, Summer 2000, p. 71.

14. Joan Gaustad, *Schools Attack the Roots of Violence*, 1991, ERIC Document Number ED 335 806.

15. Sean Kelly, "Bullying Back in Focus After California Shootings," *The Denver Post*, March 11, 2001, p. A11.

16. Steven L. Rosenberg, Loren M. McKeon, and Thomas E. Dinero, "Positive Peer Solutions," *Phi Delta Kappan*, October 1999, p. 114.

17. "About the Hands Project," n.d., <http://www.handsproject.org/home.html> (March 22, 2001).

18. Richard Danielson, "Zero Tolerance Leaves Zero Options," *St. Petersburg Times*, March 10, 2001, p. 4B.

19. Heather E. Bruce and Bryan Dexter Davis, "Slam: Hip-Hop Meets Poetry—A Strategy for Violence Intervention," *English Journal*, May 2000, pp. 119–127.

20. David Gill, "Giving Peace a Chance," *English Journal*, May 2000, pp. 74–77.

21. Reece L. Peterson and Russell Skiba, "Creating School Climates That Prevent School Violence," *Preventing School Failure*, Spring 2000, p. 122.

22. Robert M. Gladden, "The Small School Movement: A Review of the Literature," in Michelle Fine and Janis I. Somerville, eds., *Small Schools, Big Imaginations* (Chicago: Cross City Campaign for Urban School Reform, 1998), p. 116.

23. John Petrimoulx, "As Risks Rise, Children Fall Hard," *St. Petersburg Times*, March 30, 2001, p. 8B.

Books

Dorsey, Jason Ryan. *Can Students End School Violence? Solutions from America's Youth*. Nashville, Tenn.: JayMar Services, 1999.

Egendorf, Laura K., editor. *School Shootings*. San Diego, Calif.: Greenhaven Press, 2002.

Grapes, Bryan J. (ed.) *School Violence*. San Diego, Calif.: Greenhaven Press, 2000.

Hoffman, Allan M. and Randal W. Summers. *Teen Violence: A Global View*. Westport, Conn.: Greenwood Publishing Group, 2000.

Kay, Philip, Andrea Estepa, and Al Desetta (eds). *Things Get Hectic: Teens Write About the Violence That Surrounds Them*. New York: Simon & Schuster, 1998.

Kreiner, Anna. *Everything You Need to Know About School Violence*. New York: Rosen Publishing, 1996.

Internet Addresses

American Psychological Association
<http://helping.apa.org/warningsigns>

CNN: Are Our Schools Safe?
<http://www.cnn.com/SPECIALS/1998/schools>

NEA Safe Schools Now
<http://www.nea.org/issues/safescho>

Index